DR. GARY SMALLEY

P9-CDJ-941

I Promise

How 5 Commitments
Determine the Destiny
of Your Marriage

SMALL GROUP STUDY GUIDE
6 Video-Based Lessons

I Promise—Small Group Study
Copyright © 2006 Gary Smalley
Edition 1.0

All rights reserved. No part of this book may be reproduced, stored in a retrieval system, or transmitted in any form, without the written permission of Purpose Driven® Publishing.

PurposeDriven®

Published by Purpose Driven® Publishing
20 Empire
Lake Forest, CA 92630
www.purposedriven.com

The phrase Purpose Driven® is a registered trademark of Purpose Driven® Ministries.
All rights reserved.

Scripture quotations noted NLT are from THE HOLY BIBLE, NEW LIVING TRANSLATION. Copyright 1996. Used by permission of Tyndale House Publishers, Inc, Wheaton, IL 60189. All rights reserved.

Scripture quotations noted NIV are taken from the HOLY BIBLE, NEW INTERNATIONAL VERSION. Copyright 1973, 1978, and 1984 by International Bible Society. Used by permission of Zondervan Bible Publishing House. All rights reserved.

Scripture quotations noted MSG are from THE MESSAGE by Eugene H. Peterson. Copyright 1993, 1994, 1995, 1996, and 2000. Used by permission of NavPress Publishing Group. All rights reserved.

Scripture quotations noted NKJV are taken from the NEW KING JAMES VERSION. Copyright 1979, 1980, 1982 by Thomas Nelson, Inc. Used by permission. All rights reserved.

Scripture quotations noted NASB are from the NEW AMERICAN STANDARD BIBLE, 1960, 1962, 1963, 1968, 1971, 1972, 1973, 1975, 1977 by The Lockman Foundation. Used by permission.

Scripture quotations noted TEV are from TODAY'S ENGLISH VERSION (American Bible Society, 1865 Broadway, New York, NY 10023) and are used by permission.

Scripture quotations noted KJV are from THE KING JAMES VERSION.

Table of Contents

Welcome to "I Promise"

Early in my marriage, I frequently did things and said things that left my wife, Norma, feeling very unsafe in our relationship. All too often I criticized her or tried to change some area of her life I thought needed to be changed to make me happy. Instead of using my words and body language to affirm and encourage her, I often chose to nag her and frown upon her, both literally and figuratively. I excelled at making mental lists of the things I thought I needed my wife to do and to be. Self-centeredness and selfishness blinded me to the true ingredients that make for a great relationship.

I recently asked Norma to reflect on the early years of our marriage and, specifically, my actions. She used words like "critical," "controlling," "overwhelming," "workaholic," and "unrealistic expectations." "In the long run," she said, "it didn't really work for either of us . . . I loved all your dreams, but they swamped me."

Even now it's painful for me to hear how difficult I made life for this incredibly able woman God has given as my life's mate. If you are like us, you long for a marriage in which you feel secure and unconditionally loved. Current research concludes that all humans long for love from another human—to have someone to love, and to have someone love us. It is part of our innermost hardwiring. But experts are also finding that we only stay relationally connected in a fulfilling way to people with whom we feel secure and safe. When you feel safe with someone who loves you, you will open your heart to him or her, and deep friendship and intimacy will develop naturally. God designed us for deep, loving relationships; you and I just need to create a more secure place for love to flourish with our mates.

Too often you and I get hopelessly stuck, afraid to open up with our mates. We're not quite sure what our spouses will say or do when they begin to really know us; or we fear how they'll use what they learn about us. You may feel on edge with your mate, constantly worrying about when he or she will break your heart, violate your confidence, or offend you in ways that keep you feeling insecure, unsafe, or devalued.

Most of us don't have a clue about how important security is. As couples in this study, help each other remember that learning new insights about how to become a safe person will require the support and security of every member of the group. Model within your support group the security you need in your marriage.

My prayer for you is that this study will be the catalyst for a breakthrough in your marriage, wherever it is today on the journey to being great. Or if you already have a good marriage, that you will make your good marriage—GREAT!

Let's get started!

Blessings,

Gary Smalley

Acknowledgement

My first word of thanks is to God. He is so wonderful to those who seek him! I am humbled by his many rewards!

Second, I am privileged to have a Purpose Driven Pastor that I not only learn from but also consider like family. So it is with great pleasure that I dedicate this book to Pastor Ted Cunningham. With his love for Christ and willingness to assist me in helping couples around the world, this curriculum is now in your hands to use and grow as God leads you!

Third, thank you to the entire Purpose Driven team and especially Buddy Owens, John Northrup and Doug Slaybaugh for your leadership and encouragement. Buddy Owens brought excellence and depth to this project like no one else could! To my writing team and agent, Terry Brown, Ted Cunningham, Roger Gibson and Sue Parks. And finally to my precious wife, Norma, my biggest blessing from God. Thank you for allowing me to be open to others about our marriage so that we might help many others, together. I have loved our 42 years of marriage!

Understanding Your Study Guide

To do all we can to help you capture and comprehend these invaluable insights about marriage, we've created several important features to this study guide.

Looking Ahead / Catching Up: You'll open each meeting with an opportunity for everyone to check in with each other about how everyone is doing with the weekly assignments. Accountability—being there for one another—gives us a much better chance to succeed at unleashing the life-changing truths contained in this study.

Key Verse: Each week a key verse or Scripture passage establishes the theme and binds the group with the glue that is God's Word. It works best to read the passage aloud and in as many translations as your group has—the better to prompt discussion and discern the full meaning of the passage.

Video Lesson: There is a fifteen-to-twenty minute video lesson from Gary Smalley for the group to watch together each week. Take notes in the lesson outlines as you watch the videos, and refer back to these outlines during your discussion time.

Discussion Questions: After each video segment, your group can dive into one or more of several questions provided to stir group discussion and learning. Feel free to discuss as many of the questions as your group wants. The material in this study is meant to be your servant, not your master. So there's no need to rush. In fact, it's far better to give everyone ample opportunity to share their thoughts. If you don't get through all of the discussion questions, that's OK. You might consider taking them up as a couple privately, or on your own in a time of solitude.

Living on Purpose: In his book, *The Purpose Driven® Life*, Pastor Rick Warren identifies God's five purposes for our lives: They are worship, fellowship, discipleship, ministry, and evangelism. We will focus on one of these five purposes in each lesson, and see how they tie in to the subject of the study. This section really drives home the content of our study, so you'll definitely want to leave time for it as a group.

Prayer Direction: When you really stop to think about it, praying for one another, and with one another, is one of the greatest privileges of small group life. Humbly talking to Jesus about one another's needs and hopes can move us, change us, and grow us in very special ways. It's really true—so be sure to leave enough time for that, too.

Putting It Into Practice: We want to be hearers of the Word, yes, but also doers of the Word (James 1:22). This section of the study spells out the assignments we would like everyone in the group to complete before the next meeting. These activities are very practical, and will help you apply the truths you learn in each lesson to your marriages and your lives.

How to Use this Video Curriculum

Follow these four simple steps for a successful small group meeting:

1. Open your group meeting by using the "Looking Ahead" or "Catching Up" sections of your study guide.

2. Watch the video lesson together and take notes in the outlines in this study guide. Each video lesson is between fifteen and twenty minutes in length.

3. Complete the rest of the discussion materials for each session, including the "Living on Purpose" and "Prayer Direction" sections.

4. Review the "Putting It Into Practice" assignments and commit to doing them before your next meeting.

Read the Book!

To maximize the impact of this study, we recommend that each participant have a copy of both this study guide and the book *I Promise*, by Gary Smalley. Reading assignments and in-group review of chapters in the *I Promise* book are a vital part of this learning experience. The book will become a valuable permanent resource for review and sharing once the course has been completed.

Security:

THE SECRET TO
A GREAT MARRIAGE

Imagine if your home were the safest place in the world—
a place where you and your spouse had the security and
freedom to be completely open, without fear of being
criticized, blamed, or judged by each other.

LOOKING AHEAD . . . . **10 minutes**

- Welcome to *I Promise*. Take just a few minutes for everyone to introduce themselves.

- What do you want to get out of this study?

- Opening Prayer: Pray that God will strengthen you through this study as you work on freeing your marriage to be all it can be. Pray that God will begin to restore marital joy and fulfillment to those marriages that may be really hurting.

Key Verse

How precious are your thoughts about me, O God!
They are innumerable! I can't even count them;
they outnumber the grains of sand!

Psalm 139:17–18a (NLT)

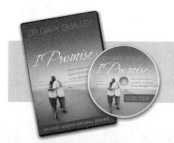

Watch the video lesson now and take notes in
the outline . . . . *20 minutes*

Security: THE SECRET TO A GREAT MARRIAGE

Security Defined:

Security is the freedom to truly open up and be known at a deep, intimate level without fear of being blamed, criticized, judged, condemned, or perhaps worst of all, deemed unacceptable.

- Security creates an environment where intimacy and deep, lasting friendship can flourish naturally and automatically.

THREE WAYS TO BUILD A SECURE MARRIAGE

1. Create safety for your mate.

- Put a deadbolt on your mouth. Stop being critical. Stop judging, condemning, and belittling.

2. Honor your mate.

- Love and value your mate as much as God does.

3. Be totally committed to your mate.

> ### Look at the value God places on your spouse!
>
> *Yet to all who received him, to those who believed in his name, he gave the right to become children of God.* (John 1:12 NIV)
>
> *How great is the love the Father has lavished on us, that we should be called children of God! And that is what we are!* (1 John 3:1 NIV)
>
> If your wife is a follower of Christ, then she is a daughter of God. If your husband is a follower of Christ, then he is a son of God . . . and God loves and values your wife or husband as a father loves and values his children. Read these verses and you'll see what I mean.
>
> *God knows everything about your husband, and he never stops thinking about him* (Psalm 139:1–18).
>
> *God has even numbered the hairs on your wife's head* (Matthew 10:29–31).
>
> *God knew your husband before he was conceived* (Jeremiah 1:4–5).
>
> *God's plan for your wife has always been filled with hope and goodwill* (Jeremiah 29:11).
>
> *God is your husband's provider and he meets all of his needs* (Matthew 6:31–33).
>
> *God sings over your wife* (Zechariah 3:17).
>
> *God carries your husband close to his heart, as a shepherd carries a lamb* (Isaiah 40:11).
>
> *God is your wife's Father, and he loves her as much as he loves his son, Jesus* (John 17:23).

DISCUSSION QUESTIONS . . . . **40 minutes**

> ### Discussion Tip:
> Be sensitive and loving to anyone who may have reservations about opening up about their life or marriage. Everyone needs to feel comfortable and secure about sharing their thoughts and feelings with the group. You may have some who have never been part of a small group. Let them know that you will allow each member to open up and share as they feel comfortable and secure.

1. What does it look like to honor one another in daily life? How could you begin to treasure your spouse in practical ways that will show them how valuable and important they are to you and just how much they really do matter?

2. Complete these statements:

   I feel the most secure in our marriage when . . .

   I feel the most insecure in our marriage when . . .

3. Think about times when you may have wrestled with any of these thoughts:

   What will he/she think if I reveal this long-hidden truth about myself?

   What will she/he say if I tell her/him what I've done?

   Will he/she just laugh or ridicule me if I reveal what I'm thinking?

We are all human and we all have secrets and deep, unspoken feelings and thoughts. How might security in your marriage—the kind of security we've been digging into in this session—give you the freedom to share your deepest feelings and disclose long-kept secrets or fears about yourself?

4. Read this passage about how we need to treat one another, and discuss what it communicates about safety and security in marriage:

> [1]"Don't pick on people, jump on their failures, criticize their faults—unless, of course, you want the same treatment. [2]That critical spirit has a way of boomeranging. [3]It's easy to see a smudge on your neighbor's face and be oblivious to the ugly sneer on your own. [4]Do you have the nerve to say, 'Let me wash your face for you,' when your own face is distorted by contempt? [5]It's this whole traveling road-show mentality all over again, playing a holier-than-thou part instead of just living your part. Wipe that ugly sneer off your own face, and you might be fit to offer a washcloth to your neighbor." (Matthew 7:1–5 MSG)

5. What does the following passage communicate about commitment?

> [4]"Haven't you read," he replied, "that at the beginning the Creator 'made them male and female,' [5]and said, 'For this reason a man will leave his father and mother and be united to his wife, and the two will become one flesh'? [6]So they are no longer two, but one. Therefore what God has joined together, let man not separate." (Matthew 19:4–6 NIV)

LIVING ON PURPOSE . . . . **10 minutes**

Fellowship

Our small groups need to be secure places for us to share. Gary challenged us in this session to deadbolt our marriages against anything that would create distrust or insecurity. In order for us to open up and share with one another in our small group, we need to have the same commitment to safety and confidentiality. Read and briefly discuss the Purpose Driven Group Guidelines on pages 74–75 of your study guide. Commit to each other that you will abide by these rules.

PRAYER DIRECTION . . . . **15 minutes**

- Take three or four minutes to write a prayer in the space below, asking God to bless your spouse. This is not a time to complain to God or to ask him to "fix" your spouse; rather, it is a time to pray for God to pour out his grace on their life. Remember, no complaining, just blessing.

- Now take three or four minutes to write a prayer in the space below, asking God to help you be a better husband or wife—and a better friend—for your spouse. Ask God to help you see and value your spouse the way he does.

- Ask couples to share prayer requests as they feel led. Be sure to record these requests in the Small Group Prayer and Praise Report section on pages 77–79 of this study guide. Then pray for each other's requests.

Putting It Into Practice

Complete these assignments before your next meeting:

1. Read chapters 1–3 in *I Promise* before your next group meeting, and be prepared to share your thoughts and insights with your group.

2. Start crafting your *I Promise* Marriage Constitution.

   For an example, Gary's *I Promise* Marriage Constitution is on page 65. When this study is finished and your Marriage Constitution is complete, please consider framing it for all to see, especially your children.

   Begin writing your own preamble to your marriage constitution in the space below. (We have included Gary's preamble as an example.)

> We want to be hearers of the Word, yes, but also doers of the Word (James 1:22). This section of the study spells out the assignments we would like everyone in the group to complete before the next meeting. These activities are very practical, and will help you apply the truths you learn in each lesson to your marriages and your lives.

GARY'S PREAMBLE:

When we wed I committed to love and cherish you all the days of my life, and I affirm that commitment today. I love you dearly, more than life itself. I honor you and place you above all other people in my life. My goal is to create in our marriage a place of safety and security in which you and I can share everything without fear, and grow together in deeper love and intimacy. To confirm my commitment to this goal, I willingly make these five solemn promises to you.

Preamble:

_____

_____

_____

_____

_____

3. Make a list of all the compelling reasons—both intangible and tangible—to stay together as a couple.

For example . . .

- God desires it
- Love can conquer all
- You will live longer (Statistics show us that women live 10 percent longer and men 23 percent longer)
- Financial impact
- The children's well-being
- The anguish and cost of a custody battle
- Impact on other family and friends—and how it will affect all future gatherings and major events in your life
- Because it's said that what we fight for in this life says a lot about us
- To keep dreams alive
- Intimacy comes through pain and a determined spirit
- Being true to our word and vows
- _____
- _____
- _____

4. Start an Honor Journal.

There is no better way to build the value of your mate into your heart than to start keeping a list of reasons you believe your mate is so valuable. The longer the list, the more valuable he or she will become.

Gary has compiled four and a half pages of qualities, actions, physical characteristics, attitudes, behaviors, character traits, memories, gifts received, and so on about why his wife is so incredibly important to him.

Here are a few practical suggestions for getting started:

a. Become a student of your mate. Be attentive to his or her preferences: favorite food, favorite kind of date, best idea of a vacation, most relaxing activity, most fun activity, etc. Sadly, many husbands and wives cannot tell you about each other's tastes and preferences.

b. Do sweat the small stuff. Husbands and wives sometimes make the mistake of thinking of honor as being only the big things they do for each other. Write down a few simple things that would show honor to your spouse, i.e., holding hands, flowers, listening, small gifts, sunset walks, etc.

c. List your mate's positive qualities. Make a list of all the things you admire about him or her. Post these in a highly visible place in your home where you both can see them every day. A written list, instead of just mental notes, has a way of making the good things about your mate seem all the more special.

d. Be a student of your actions this week, both positive and negative. Take special note of those actions that create security in your marriage.

What's Next

In the next five sessions, Gary will share five promises to help you create a Marriage Security System. Each of these five promises is designed to promote security and to lead your marriage into deeper love and intimacy. When you read and apply these promises, you will discover the way to create a secure place in your marriage.*

In our next session, we will look at the 1st Promise: *I promise to conform my beliefs to God's truths.* This first promise will help you to . . .

> . . . *stop complaining about your spouse;*

> . . . *stop judging your spouse;*

> . . . *stop trying to change your mate or anyone else who bugs you.*

---

* *For more information about "safety" see Chapter 5 in* **The DNA of Relationships** *by Gary Smalley.*

SESSION TWO

1st Promise:
I PROMISE TO CONFORM MY BELIEFS TO GOD'S TRUTHS

Think about living a life where you hide God's Word in your heart each day, and little by little it changes how you think, how you feel, and how you act toward your mate.

CATCHING UP . . . . **10 minutes**

- Opening Prayer: Ask God to use this session to deepen your appreciation of your spouse and teach you new ways to show love and honor to your mate.

- Did you read chapters 1–3 in *I Promise* this week? One or two of you share something you read that was particularly meaningful to you.

- Did you complete the preamble of your *I Promise* Marriage Constitution? If so, would anyone like to share it with the group?

- Did you start your Honor Journal? It would be great if some of you shared one or two ideas from your journal with the group.

Key Verse

Above all else, guard your heart, for it is the wellspring of life.

Proverbs 4:23 (NIV)

Watch the video lesson now and take notes in the outline . . . . *20 minutes*

1st Promise: I PROMISE TO CONFORM MY BELIEFS TO GOD'S TRUTHS

- All escalated arguments are really just your attempt to change your mate and their attempt to change you.

- All addictions are nothing more than a person trying to medicate the pain they are having with weak relationships.

- Here's the secret: It is not what happens to you that determines your happiness or your quality of life. Your quality of life comes directly from the beliefs you have in your heart.

Above all else, guard your heart, for it is the wellspring of life.

(Proverbs 4:23 NIV)

For as he thinks in his heart, so is he.

(Proverbs 23:7 NKJV)

[18] "But evil words come from an evil heart and defile the person who says them. [19] For from the heart come evil thoughts, murder, adultery, all other sexual immorality, theft, lying, and slander. [20a] These are what defile you . . ."

(Matthew 15:18–20a NLT)

I have hidden your word in my heart, that I might not sin against you.

(Psalm 119:11 NLT)

⁹For if you confess with your mouth that Jesus is Lord and believe in your heart that God raised him from the dead, you will be saved. ¹⁰For it is by believing in your heart that you are made right with God, and it is by confessing with your mouth that you are saved.

(Romans 10:9–10 NLT)

Search me, O God, and know my heart; test me and know my anxious thoughts.

(Psalm 139:23 NIV)

FOUR WAYS TO GUARD YOUR HEART

1. Identify any area in your life that does not reflect God's love.

For example . . . Thoughts of: Lust, Envy, Arrogance, Vanity.
Feelings of: Rage, Contempt, Indifference, Selfishness.

For you have been called to live in freedom—not freedom to satisfy your sinful nature, but freedom to serve one another in love.

(Galatians 5:13 NLT)

³⁷Jesus replied, "'You must love the Lord your God with all your heart, all your soul, and all your mind.' ³⁸This is the first and greatest commandment. ³⁹A second is equally important: 'Love your neighbor as yourself.' ⁴⁰All the other commandments and all the demands of the prophets are based on these two commandments."

(Matthew 22:37–40 NLT)

2. Find a Bible verse that addresses the behavior that needs to change.

3. Memorize the verse.

4. Repeat the verse in your mind several times a day.

Do not conform any longer to the pattern of this world, but be transformed by the renewing of your mind.

(Romans 12:2a NIV)

Repeat them again and again to your children. Talk about them when you are at home and when you are away on a journey, when you are lying down and when you are getting up again.

(Deuteronomy 6:7 NLT)

. . . Everyone should be quick to listen, slow to speak and slow to become angry.

(James 1:19b NIV)

8And now, dear brothers and sisters, let me say one more thing as I close this letter. Fix your thoughts on what is true and honorable and right. Think about things that are pure and lovely and admirable. Think about things that are excellent and worthy of praise. 9Keep putting into practice all you learned from me and heard from me and saw me doing, and the God of peace will be with you. (Philippians 4:8–9 NLT)

- Guard your heart, above all other things, because out of it comes who you are.

DISCUSSION QUESTIONS . . . . **30 minutes**

1. Choose one Scripture passage from this session to memorize this week. How might this passage keep you from complaining, criticizing, or trying to change your mate?

2. Gary stated: "It is not what happens to you that determines your happiness or your quality of life. Your quality of life comes directly from the beliefs you have in your heart." How does that statement apply to your marriage?

3. What are some practical steps you can take to live out the simple but profound wisdom of James 1:19b?

Everyone should be quick to listen, slow to speak and slow to become angry . . .

(James 1:19b NIV)

4. How can the practice of hiding God's Word in your heart help you monitor your beliefs and create security in your marriage?

LIVING ON PURPOSE . . . . **15 minutes**

DISCIPLESHIP

When Jesus prayed for his disciples, he also prayed for *future believers*. He stressed the importance of Scripture in setting you and me apart for his special purpose: *"Sanctify them by the truth; your word is truth"* (John 17:17 NIV). As followers of Christ, we are committed to comprehending every aspect of the Bible so we may be prepared *in every way, fully equipped for every good thing God wants [us] to do* (2 Timothy 3:17 NLT).

Understanding the full dimension of the Bible includes hearing, reading, studying, memorizing, meditating, and applying Scripture.

How would you describe your grasp on the Bible?

❑ All the Bible I get is usually just at church.

❑ I try to pick up my Bible and take in a few verses each week.

❑ I use study tools (study Bible, concordance, etc.).

❑ I am already memorizing Scripture as part of my regular routine.

❑ I am repeating verses to myself until they sink into my heart.

Memorizing and meditating on Scripture can be a difficult challenge. But when you begin hiding God's Word in your heart, you will see your beliefs start to change. You'll know your beliefs are changing, because your behavior will start changing. Then, you're on your way to becoming like Jesus little by little as you hide his words in your heart.

PRAYER DIRECTION . . . . **10 minutes**

• Pray that God will help each of you develop a deeper hunger and a stronger discipline to hide his Word in your hearts.

• Ask couples to share prayer requests as they feel led. Be sure to record these requests in the Small Group Prayer and Praise Report section on pages 77–79 of this study guide. Then pray for each other's requests.

Putting It Into Practice

1. Read chapter 4 in *I Promise* before your next group meeting, and be prepared to share your thoughts about what you read.

2. You were asked in the first discussion question to choose a Bible passage to memorize this week. Write the passage you have chosen on a 3x5 card, sticky note, or computer screen saver. Read it each morning and glance at it from time to time throughout your day.

3. Begin writing Article I of your *I Promise* Marriage Constitution. (We have included Gary's as an example on the next page.) Tell your spouse in your own words how you have a new appreciation for how God's Word, hidden in your heart, can enrich your marriage and relationship. Promise your spouse you will monitor your deepest beliefs and have the humility to change your beliefs when they do not conform to God's truths. This promise will be a giant step in bringing security to your marriage.

I promise . . .
_____

_____

_____

_____

_____

_____

_____

_____

_____

_____

_____

GARY'S ARTICLE I

I PROMISE to conform my beliefs to God's truth. I will gain control of my outlook, emotions, and happiness by continually examining my deepest beliefs and striving to make them consistent with what God's Word says. I take sole responsibility for my beliefs with the understanding that they, not you, determine my emotions, words, thoughts, and actions. Thus I lift from you the burden of being responsible for any of my ultimate life quality.

What's Next

The next promise will guide you to the only source capable of providing fulfillment, inner peace, and contentment. And here's a hint—that source is not your spouse. Next week's session will take a huge burden off of you and your mate, and infuse your marriage with a mega dose of security.

Notes

SESSION THREE

2nd Promise:
I PROMISE TO BE
FILLED BY GOD

What if you focused on God every day

to meet your deepest needs,

instead of waiting on your mate to complete you?

CATCHING UP . . . . 10 minutes

- How did memorizing and meditating on Scripture this past week affect your marriage and daily routine? How challenging was it—given all of life's demands—to remember the verses "day and night"?

- Did you all write the first article of your marriage constitutions? Would anyone like to share what they wrote?

- Did you get a chance to read chapter 4 in *I Promise*? Take a few minutes to share your thoughts and insights.

- Opening Prayer: Ask God to open your ears and your hearts to what he wants to say to you in this session.

Key Verse

Without faith it is impossible to please God, because anyone who comes to him must believe that he exists and he rewards those who earnestly seek him.

Hebrews 11:6 (NIV)

Watch the video lesson now and take notes in the outline . . . . 20 minutes

2nd Promise: I PROMISE TO BE FILLED BY GOD

WHERE DO I LOOK FOR FULFILLMENT IN LIFE?

1. People will not fill me up.

(examples: your mate, children, friends)

2. Places will not fill me up.

(example: your home, exclusive neighborhood, vacations, etc.)

3. Things will not fill me up.

(example: your job, money, cars, toys, success)

- People, places, and things will not fill you up. Instead, allow God to fill you up to all the fullness of himself.

KEY BELIEFS ABOUT GOD TO HIDE IN YOUR HEART

1. God exists and rewards me as I diligently seek him.

> *And without faith it is impossible to please God, because anyone who comes to him must believe that he exists and that he rewards those who earnestly seek him.*

(Hebrews 11:6 NIV)

2. God meets all of my deepest needs.

> *And my God will meet all your needs according to his glorious riches in Christ Jesus.*

(Philippians 4:19 NIV)

> *"But seek first the kingdom of God and His righteousness, and all these things shall be added to you."*

(Matthew 6:33 NKJV)

3. God fills me with himself.

- Through his Spirit, I have access to an inexhaustible supply of love, an abundant life, and an unending source of fulfillment and perspective.

FIVE KEY PASSAGES TO HIDE IN YOUR HEART

¹⁶I pray that out of his glorious riches he may strengthen you with power through his Spirit in your inner being, ¹⁷so that Christ may dwell in your hearts through faith. And I pray that you, being rooted and established in love, ¹⁸may have power, together with all the saints, to grasp how wide and long and high and deep is the love of Christ, ¹⁹and to know this love that surpasses knowledge—that you may be filled to the measure of all the fullness of God . . . ²⁰who is able to do immeasurably more than all we ask or imagine, according to his power that is at work within us . . .

(Ephesians 3:16–20 NIV)

¹Since, then, you have been raised with Christ, set your hearts on things above, where Christ is seated at the right hand of God. ²Set your minds on things above, not on earthly things. ³For you died, and your life is now hidden with Christ in God . . . ⁵Put to death, therefore, whatever belongs to your earthly nature: sexual immorality, impurity, lust, evil desires and greed, which is idolatry . . . ⁷You used to walk in these ways, in the life you once lived. ⁸But now you must rid yourselves of all such things as these: anger, rage, malice, slander, and filthy language from your lips. ⁹Do not lie to each other, since you have taken off your old self with its practices ¹⁰and have put on the new self, which is being renewed in knowledge in the image of its Creator . . . ¹²Therefore, as God's chosen people, holy and dearly loved, clothe yourselves with compassion, kindness, humility, gentleness and patience. ¹³Bear with each other and forgive whatever grievances you may have against one another. Forgive as the Lord forgave you. ¹⁴And over all these virtues put on love, which binds them all together in perfect unity. ¹⁵Let the peace of Christ rule in your hearts, since as members of one body you were called to peace. And be thankful. ¹⁶Let the word of Christ dwell in you richly as you teach and admonish one another with all wisdom, and as you sing psalms, hymns and spiritual songs with gratitude in your hearts to God. ¹⁷And whatever you do, whether in word or deed, do it all in the name of the Lord Jesus, giving thanks to God the Father through him.

(Colossians 3:1–17 NIV)

⁹That if you confess with your mouth, "Jesus is Lord," and believe in your heart that God raised him from the dead, you will be saved. ¹⁰For it is with your heart that you believe and are justified, and it is with your mouth that you confess and are saved.

(Romans 10:9–10 NIV)

³We can rejoice, too, when we run into problems and trials, for we know that they are good for us—they help us learn to endure. ⁴And endurance develops strength of character in us, and character strengthens our confident expectation of salvation. ⁵And this expectation will not disappoint us. For we know how dearly God loves us, because he has given us the Holy Spirit to fill our hearts with his love.

(Romans 5:3–5 NLT)

You, my brothers, were called to be free. But do not use your freedom to indulge the sinful nature; rather, serve one another in love.

(Galatians 5:13 NIV)

Note from Gary: After I memorized these sections of Scripture, repeating these verses back to God over and over for weeks, I began to experience a powerful freedom from sexual lust, impurity, greed, and other pleasure seeking thoughts and actions. With his power in me, I have found the emotions of anger, rage, malice, slander, and filthy language diminishing from my life. And I am finding that he is renewing me day after day and transforming me into his image. I may never be a "saint," but I am finding his words coming alive within me and proving for me how powerful his Word and Spirit are as they live inside of you and me.

DISCUSSION QUESTIONS . . . . **40 minutes**

1. In the past, where have you turned to find happiness and purpose?

2. What unrealistic expectations for life or your personal fulfillment might you be placing on your mate? If you are not married, what steps can you take in this area to prepare yourself for marriage?

3. When your mate fails to measure up to your expectations, how are your thoughts and emotions impacted? How do you usually react when this happens? How does your reaction affect your spouse?

4. What steps can you take to reduce the expectations you place on your mate?

Note from Gary: This area is so critical. It took me awhile to capture its impact. But, remember, you can't change your mate, but only influence him or her by your own commitment to making changes. As you become more and more like Christ by his power within you, your mate will see and experience it through you. They will feel more secure with you and will usually want what you have. But if you continually try to correct or criticize your mate, you will only add to an insecure, unsafe, and exasperating home. If you desire a satisfying marriage—and we all yearn for that—then resist those impulses to be critical. Instead, choose the way of love by searching for changes you could make. Be consistent in doing this, and you'll likely be stunned at how quickly your spouse will notice and begin to do likewise.

LIVING ON PURPOSE . . . . 10 minutes

WORSHIP

Christ is our Creator and Sustainer:

> *¹⁵He is the image of the invisible God, the firstborn over all creation. ¹⁶For by him all things were created: things in heaven and on earth, visible and invisible, whether thrones or powers or rulers or authorities; all things were created by him and for him. ¹⁷He is before all things, and in him all things hold together.* (Colossians 1:15–17 NIV)

God created your life and he is the sustaining force in your life, not your mate. The very breath you take this moment is a gift from him. Maybe you see him as the source for the miracle of your birth, but not as the source for your happiness and contentment in the details of everyday life. Maybe too many of your assumptions about happiness rest on the weary shoulders of your mate.

Read this admonition from the apostle Paul:

> *So here's what I want you to do, God helping you: Take your everyday, ordinary life—your sleeping, eating, going-to-work, and walking-around life—and place it before God as an offering. Embracing what God does for you is the best thing you can do for him.* (Romans 12:1 MSG)

Do you view your life as an offering to God? Do you look at your marriage as an offering to God? Do you seek God in order to be filled—to the point of "overflowing?" How might your life be different if you approached your marriage every day as an act of worship?

PRAYER DIRECTION . . . . 10 minutes

1. Before you pray, have five volunteers read aloud the Five Key Passages to Hide in Your Heart from this week's video outline.

2. Pray for one another to work hard to establish God as your primary source of life. Ask God to encourage each member as they let go of expectations from this earth and turn them over to him. Releasing your mate from your expectations is like setting a prisoner free. Pray that God will "free" the members of your group.

3. Take some time to pray for the hurting marriages in your group—that they will receive patience and understanding while God fills each person to the fullness of Christ (see Ephesians 5:17).

Putting It Into Practice

1. Read chapter 5 in *I Promise* before your next group meeting, and be prepared to share your thoughts about what you read.

2. Complete Article II of your *I Promise* Marriage Constitution. (We have included Gary's as an example below.)

I promise . . .

_____

_____

_____

_____

_____

_____

GARY'S ARTICLE II

I PROMISE to be filled by God. I will keep God in my heart as my source of joy and love. My love for you will be his love flowing through me. And I will receive your love as overflow from him. I will base the security of our marriage on making Christ my boss. I will strive to conform to his image and follow all his commands, especially the one to love you and care for you all the days of my life. (Ephesians 5:25–26; Philippians 4:19)

---

3. Each day this week, take five-to-ten minutes with your spouse to read and discuss a different passage from Gary's list of Five Key Passages to Hide in Your Heart.

4. The assessment on the following page will help you get an idea of how safe your spouse might feel with you. After you have tallied your results, look back at the answers to identify actions you are taking that may be hindering security. Then, reflect on these actions and ask God about them before approaching your mate. After you have prayed, take a step of faith by talking to your spouse about your self-assessment. You may have identified character flaws in your life that need healing and attention. You may also have identified ways you have wounded your mate. If so, seek forgiveness. Being contrite, saying you're sorry and asking for forgiveness will, over time, leaven your marriage with a life-giving sense of security.

HOW DO YOU KNOW IF YOUR SPOUSE FEELS SAFE WITH YOU?

Use this scale

5—All the time; **4**—Often; **3**—Regularly but infrequently; **2**—Only once in awhile; **1**—Never

1. _____ I judge or criticize him/her.

2. _____ I neglect to show him/her how interesting he/she is to me, and I'm not curious to understand him/her.

3. _____ I blame him/her for how I feel when he/she offends me or hurts my feelings.

4. _____ I lash out at him/her whenever I am feeling unfulfilled or unhappy.

5. _____ I make it difficult for him/her to open up and share his/her deepest feelings, suggestions, and needs with me.

6. _____ When I hear an idea or thought from him/her, my first response is to be critical and/or find fault.

7. _____ I neglect to show concern about every area of his/her life.

8. _____ I underestimate his/her value and do not place him/her high enough on my priority list.

9. _____ I sense he/she seems to be tense spending time with me.

10. _____ I neglect to value his/her opinions, ideas, concerns, expectations, and feelings.

11. _____ I neglect to consider his/her unique physical, mental, emotional, and spiritual makeup.

12. _____ I hesitate to trust his/her words and actions daily.

13. _____ I have a tendency to want to control or influence how he/she feels about himself/herself.

14. _____ I neglect to praise him/her for what he/she does and says.

15. _____ I neglect to repair relational damage quickly.

16. _____ My anger is out of control with him/her.

17. _____ I neglect to partner with him/her in finding win-win solutions to mutual problems or disagreements.

18. _____ I don't see him/her as a team player.

19. _____ I don't work very hard to have a loving and fulfilling marriage.

20. _____ I have a hard time forgiving him/her when he/she offends me.

Scoring:

20–40   Your mate probably feels safe with you much of the
              time. (The goal is to hit 20.)

41–70   You need to work on some key things for your mate
              to feel safe with you.

71–100   It's very likely your mate generally feels unsafe
              with you.

Remember, the safer each person feels in a marriage, the greater the sense of satisfaction and fulfillment both will feel in what is the most important relationship in our entire lives.

What's Next

How you handle irritations will determine the level of security in your marriage. In the next session we will be challenged to be more positive and encouraging with our mates, and to better manage minor irritations and disappointments by turning them into blessings.

Notes

SESSION FOUR

3rd Promise:
I PROMISE TO FIND GOD'S BEST IN EVERY TRIAL

What difference could it make if you saw every trial and irritation that comes from your spouse as an opportunity for you to become more like Christ?

CATCHING UP . . . . **10 minutes**

• Opening Prayer

• Did you get a chance to read chapter 5 in *I Promise*? Take a few minutes to share your thoughts and insights.

• How did you do on the self-assessment inventory indicating how safe your spouse might feel with you? How do you feel about your score?

Key Verse

We can rejoice, too, when we run into problems and trials, for we know that they are good for us—they help us learn to endure.

Romans 5:3 (NLT)

Watch the video lesson now and take notes in the outline . . . . *20 minutes*

3rd Promise: I PROMISE TO FIND GOD'S BEST IN EVERY TRIAL

FOUR WAYS TO CHANGE YOUR BELIEFS ABOUT TRIALS AND IRRITATIONS

1. Be quick to listen.

> *. . . Everyone should be quick to listen, slow to speak and slow to become angry.*
>
> (James 1:19b NIV)

Keys to Great Listening

- Listen slow, not fast

- Listen until you understand

- Anger is the seed of love

> **Note from Gary:** You become angry when you perceive you are losing or not getting something important. So, anger often is rooted in disappointment. Dealing with this disappointment in a thoughtful way can be a spring for increased sensitivity, compassion, and mutual understanding, which in turn are the basic ingredients of love.
>
> Even though trials bring pain they can be the best source of our growth and maturity. When we give God thanks for trials, we surrender to God's refining process. He uses the fire of trials to make us like pure gold, until we become a reflection of his love. A great way to respond to trials is to write down the benefits of the pain. (See chapter 6 in the *I Promise* book for illustrations.)

2. Humble yourself.

- Recognize your helplessness.

    . . . God opposes the proud but gives grace to the humble.

    (James 4:6b NIV)

- Sometimes, a great prayer is, "God, help me with the things I cannot help myself with."

3. Give God thanks in all circumstances.

Give thanks in all circumstances, for this is God's will for you in Christ Jesus.

(1 Thessalonians 5:18 NIV)

Keys to Gratefulness

- Gratefulness is an antidote for complaining.

And we know that God causes everything to work together for the good of those who love God and are called according to his purpose for them.

(Romans 8:28 NLT)

- Identify the log in your own eye.

"And why worry about a speck in your friend's eye when you have a log in your own?"

(Matthew 7:3 NLT)

4. Wait until God's Word takes root in your heart.

9"My gracious favor is all you need. My power works best in your weakness." So now I am glad to boast about my weaknesses, so that the power of Christ may work through me. 10Since I know it is all for Christ's good, I am quite content with my weaknesses and with insults, hardships, persecutions, and calamities. For when I am weak, then I am strong.

(2 Corinthians 12:9–10 NLT)

Consider it pure joy, my brothers, whenever you face trials of many kinds.

(James 1:2 NIV)

3We can rejoice, too, when we run into problems and trials, for we know that they are good for us—they help us learn to endure. 4And endurance develops strength of character in us, and character strengthens our confident expectation of salvation. 5And this expectation will not disappoint us. For we know how dearly God loves us, because he has given us the Holy Spirit to fill our hearts with his love.

(Romans 5:3–5 NLT)

- Hide God's Word in your heart. And then watch yourself, little by little, become more grateful, until you can actually say, "Thank you," to God and to your spouse whenever you face trials and irritations. Now that's spiritual growth!

DISCUSSION QUESTIONS . . . . **40 minutes**

1. Why is it that our mate's minor faults can be so obvious to us, but our own shortcomings can remain so hidden?

2. What is your response to Gary's challenge to say "Thank you" to God when something irritates or aggravates you?

3. Jesus said in Matthew 7:3 (NLT), *"And why worry about a speck in your friend's eye when you have a log in your own?"* It's often the case that what bothers us about our spouse is really an indication of a flaw or weakness in our own character. How have you seen this to be the case in your own life and marriage?

4. How might you go about sharing thoughts of genuine appreciation with your mate when something takes place that aggravates you? Does it seem unrealistic to you to express gratitude to your spouse when you are irritated with him or her? How would your perspective need to change in order for you to be genuinely grateful and to see your irritation in a positive light?

LIVING ON PURPOSE . . . . 15 minutes

EVANGELISM

Gratitude for trials and aggravations? Honesty about your own short-comings? Security in your marriage? Is any of this really possible? Not without God's strength; and it is impossible to have God's strength without surrendering your life to him. Living a surrendered life is the only way to live a victorious life. Yes, that seems backward, maybe even nonsensical, but it is the truth. Jesus said, *"Apart from me you can do nothing"* (John 15:5 NIV). But the Bible also says, *I can do all things through Christ who strengthens me* (Philippians 4:13 NKJV). If you try to do this without Christ, you will fall flat on your face. If you have never surrendered your life to Christ and received his gift of forgiveness, now is the time to do it. Your life depends on it. Your marriage depends on it.

Take a few minutes with your group right now to watch the brief video clip by Pastor Rick Warren titled "How to Become a Follower of Christ." We have included it on your DVD.

PRAYER DIRECTION . . . . 10 minutes

- Take a moment to pray with anyone who expressed a desire to become a follower of Jesus Christ.

- Pray a prayer of personal responsibility. Ask God to help you make the necessary changes in your character by allowing his Spirit to take control and by hiding his words in your heart. Doing so will carve a path to newfound positive attitudes and behaviors for you and your spouse.

- Invite couples to share prayer requests as they feel led. Be sure to record these requests in the Small Group Prayer and Praise Report section on pages 77–79 of this study guide. Then pray for each other's requests.

Putting It Into Practice

1. Read chapter 6 in *I Promise* before your next group meeting, and be prepared to share your thoughts about what you read.

2. Complete Article III of your *I Promise* Marriage Constitution. (We have included Gary's as an example below.)

   I promise . . .

   _____

   _____

   _____

   _____

   _____

   _____

   ### GARY'S ARTICLE III

   I PROMISE to find God's best in every trial. I give you the security of knowing that the negative things that happen in our marriage will not destroy my love for you. I will not expect perfection from you, but will use even the irritations between us as opportunities to see my blind spots and foster my personal growth. I will call on the power of Christ to root out my weaknesses. (Romans 8:28; James 1:12; Romans 5:3–5)

   ---

3. Express gratitude this week to God for bringing your spouse into your life to help you become the best you can be.

4. Pray for wisdom and maybe even seek counsel from some close friends in dealing with the "logs" you find in your own eyes.

What's Next

Imagine your spouse saying to you, "Honey, from now on, I want to help you win every argument, no matter what issue we are facing. And, could I ask you to help me win at the same time?" That is the beauty of harmony and oneness in marriage. We'll talk about it in the next session.

SESSION FIVE

4th Promise:
I PROMISE TO LISTEN AND COMMUNICATE WITH LOVE

What would it be like to face every marital conflict with the
common goal to find solutions that honor each other's needs?

CATCHING UP . . . . 10 minutes

- Opening Prayer

- Did you get a chance to read chapter 6 in *I Promise*? Take a few minutes to share your thoughts and insights.

- How did the truths you learned about irritations in our last session impact your life this past week?

- Would anyone like to share with the group how this study has reshaped and impacted your marriage so far?

Key Verse

Do not let any unwholesome talk come out of your mouths,
but only what is helpful in building others up according to their needs,
that it may benefit those who listen.

Ephesians 4:29 (NIV)

Watch the video lesson now and take notes in the outline . . . . 20 minutes

4th Promise: I PROMISE TO LISTEN AND COMMUNICATE WITH LOVE

SIX LEVELS OF COMMUNICATION

1. Small Talk

2. Sharing Facts

3. Opinions

> *Do not get drunk on wine . . . Instead, be filled with the Spirit.*
>
> (Ephesians 5:18 NIV)

Notice that the following verses apply *after* we are filled with his Spirit.

> *²¹Submit to one another out of reverence for Christ. ²²Wives, submit to your husbands as to the Lord . . . ²⁵Husbands, love your wives, just as Christ loved the church and gave himself up for her . . .*
>
> (Ephesians 5:21–25 NIV)

> *I have been crucified with Christ and I no longer live, but Christ lives in me. The life I live in the body, I live by faith in the Son of God, who loved me and gave himself for me.*
>
> (Galatians 2:20 NIV)

4. Feelings

5. Needs

6. Beliefs

THREE WAYS TO HELP YOUR MATE WIN EVERY ARGUMENT

1. Listen carefully and compassionately to their feelings, needs, and beliefs. Honor each other by taking turns listening, and don't interrupt until you fully understand your mate. Then, after you've given your spouse your full attention and empathy, share your feelings, needs, and beliefs.

2. Seek to deeply understand their feelings, needs, and beliefs. Ask your mate to let you know when he/she thinks you've demonstrated a full understanding of him/her. As you are listening, stop him/her from time to time in order to repeat back what you've heard, so you can assure and be assured you fully understand what's being said.

3. Suggest resolutions and desires for next-steps only after you both agree you understand one another. Avoid judging each other's suggested solutions. This is extremely important for establishing security and safety. Sometimes, off-the-wall suggestions can lead to a solution you both love. That's win-win and it greatly elevates the level of security in the marriage.

DISCUSSION QUESTIONS . . . . 40 minutes

LET'S DISCUSS IN DEPTH THE SIX LEVELS OF COMMUNICATION

1. Small Talk

Definition—Shallow conversation or clichés.

Examples: "How are you doing?"

"I'm fine."

"Please pass the salt."

As you can see, at this level, you learn next to nothing about life or one another. This is the lowest level of intimacy. This type of communication requires little concentration or effort, and provides about as much in relational connection and bonding.

QUESTION: Can you think of any reasons why a couple would get "stuck" at this first level and avoid going deeper in their communication?

2. Sharing Facts

Here, the couple exchanges basic facts about themselves or life in general. There's not much risk of conflict or argument—but, again, not much capacity for meaningful connection either.

Examples: "It was sure hot today, wasn't it?"

"Can you believe what the President did today!"

We have a tendency to avoid "facts" that could lead to conflict, especially when we're tired or distracted. This level of conversation generally stays friendly and safe. And there's a lot to be said for friendship communication. It seldom escalates into argument.

QUESTION: Why do you think there is little risk for an argument at this level? When do "facts" become unsafe?

3. Opinions

In this sphere of communication, couples can explore their concerns and expectations. While it opens the door for disagreement, it also opens the door for greater intimacy, closeness, and security.

Examples: "You never listen to me."

"You're wrong and you know it."

"You told me before we married that my mother was always welcome in our home."

Statements like these can actually act as portals to deep levels of communication and intimacy. By applying just a little communication skill, sifting through differences of opinion can boost you to higher planes of understanding.

But it is absolutely essential that you remember the role of the Holy Spirit in facilitating open, loving, and peaceful communication.

QUESTION: How can you reduce the risk of conflict at this level?

4. Feelings

In the fourth level of communication, a couple feels safe to share their deepest feelings and aspirations, and they treat each other's feelings and hopes with respect and care.

Examples: "Tell me if this is right, you feel afraid for our daughter because she is getting her driver's license."

"It's not that you mind me watching TV, it's that you feel cheated that we don't spend more time together."

"I could be way off, but I feel sad when my parents don't come by and see us like they used to."

This level of conversation is marked by an atmosphere of honor and mutual admiration and affection. The listener tries to understand and validate what is being communicated.

QUESTION: What does a "judgment-free zone" look like for you at this fourth level? How can you create that for your mate?

5. Needs

When a person feels safe to share his or her own deepest needs and innermost vulnerabilities, security is paramount. In addition, when one person expresses his or her deep needs, they must be met with understanding and compassion.

Examples: "See if this is right. You need some alone time at night after work and it's not that you don't want time with me, it's that you need to recoup?"

"Are you saying you need more tenderness when we talk? Describe tenderness. What does it look like to you?"

"Wait a minute, I don't understand. Am I getting this right, you're saying that we need to be saving more each month? Why? And what does that mean to you?"

Since feelings reflect whether a person's needs are being met, a couple can honor each other as they move through the fourth level (feelings) into the fifth level (needs). For example, if a person has a need to be treated with tenderness, one might see expressions of frustration or hurt on the face of the offended person. Honor, at the fifth level of intimacy, would nudge us toward asking the offended person to reveal what is needed. If an environment of safety were established, he or she could express the need for more tenderness.

QUESTION: How often do you and your mate experience this level in a secure setting?

6. Beliefs

The Bible implores us to, above all else, guard our hearts (Proverbs 4:23). Since our heart is the seat of our core beliefs, sharing these beliefs with one another achieves the deepest level of communication.

Many of our beliefs can be traced back to our childhoods and family histories. By mutually communicating and exploring your different beliefs, you find out who each of you really is and why you each act the way you do in certain situations, especially under duress and pressure. Understanding each other's beliefs and the seeds of those beliefs can impart deep, profound understanding of one another and it will empower and compel you to deal with your differences with love and gentleness.

An example: A person might realize: "When I was young, I can remember my dad telling me that no one can be trusted. 'Watch out,' he would say. 'Be careful, because people will let you down. Don't depend on anyone.'" And then, they might tell their spouse: "Now, can you see why I have trouble at times trusting you? I'm sure I have a huge core belief that people are unsafe and can't be trusted." Then, they might decide for themselves they want to learn to trust more and say to their mate: "I want these verses to seep into my heart: 'God causes all things to work together for my good because I love him and I am doing his purpose of loving others, and that includes you' (Romans 8:28). Therefore, 'I will use my new freedom in Christ to serve you in love.' I don't want to use you for my pleasure" (Galatians 5:13).

QUESTION: Is communicating at this most intimate level possible without God? How can God's Word shape your beliefs and build security into your marriage?

LIVING ON PURPOSE . . . . **10 minutes**

FELLOWSHIP

> *Be devoted to one another in brotherly love. Honor one another above yourselves.*
>
> (Romans 12:10 NIV)

> *We know what real love is because Christ gave up his life for us. And so we also ought to give up our lives for our Christian brothers and sisters.*
>
> (1 John 3:16 NLT)

> *"By this all men will know that you are my disciples, if you love one another."*
>
> (John 13:35 NIV)

True biblical fellowship is much more than small talk. It involves deep communication and honest sharing of struggles, fears, and heartaches. It involves partnering with at least one trusted friend, not to gossip with, but to pray with; not to complain to, but to encourage. It involves locking arms and joining hands with a spiritual partner—a fellow Christ-follower who is committed to your spiritual growth and well-being.

This marriage study will be finished in just one more session. But, of course, your progress toward a more secure and rewarding marriage is just getting started. It will be important for each of you to find a spiritual partner (someone of the same sex) with whom you can meet on a weekly basis for prayer and encouragement, and to hold each other accountable to follow through on the commitments you have made during this study.

In the space below, write the names of one or two people you would consider asking to be your spiritual partner. Then make a plan to call or e-mail them within the next twenty-four hours.

_____   _____
Name   Name

PRAYER DIRECTION . . . . **10 minutes**

- God loves his family. We are called to love one another as Christ loves us. Pray that your love for one another will express itself this week in loving actions.

- Invite couples to share prayer requests as they feel led. Be sure to record these requests in the Small Group Prayer and Praise Report section on pages 77–79 of this study guide. Then pray for each other's requests.

Putting It Into Practice

1. Read chapter 7 in *I Promise* before your next group meeting, and be prepared to share your thoughts about what you read.

2. Complete Article IV of your *I Promise* Marriage Constitution. (We have included Gary's as an example on the next page.)

   I promise . . .

   _____

   _____

   _____

   _____

   _____

   _____

   _____

   _____

> **GARY'S ARTICLE IV**
>
> **I PROMISE to listen and communicate with love.** I will value every word you speak as a window to your heart. I will honor your opinions, feelings, needs, and beliefs so that you will feel free to speak honestly and openly with full security in my love for you. I will be open with you in communicating my heart and will consider your feelings and needs in all my words. I will help you solve every disagreement with me until you feel like a winner. (Ephesians 4:29)

3. Practice effective communication this week. Spend some time with your mate intentionally seeking to communicate better about a subject on which you currently disagree. Use the following checklist as your guide:

- **Use and read body language.** Face your mate as you talk. If you are sitting, turn your chair toward him or her and relax. It's best to unfold your arms and legs; folded limbs send a subliminal message of being on guard or closed-minded. Unfolded limbs signal you are welcoming the other person inside your space and are interested in them and what they're saying.

- **As you talk, study your mate's posture and facial expressions.** Are the lips open? That indicates receptivity to what you're saying. Are they tightly pursed? You may be meeting resistance. Notice the hands and arms. If the hands are clenched or the arms folded, your mate may be distracted or closed off. If they are relaxed, you are probably being heard. Sometimes these body signals can tell you things that words cannot. As you observe body language, ask: What is she or he really saying? Is he or she on board with what I'm asking? You might say, "I noticed you looked away when I mentioned tightening our budget. What's on your mind? What are your thoughts?" You want to gain the most complete understanding you can. Learning to use and read facial expressions and body signals can do wonders for your ability to connect.

- **Use encouraging signals.** Nods and acknowledging words let your mate know you are listening actively. It doesn't take much; a simple "Yes," "Uh-huh," or "I see" usually suffices. It indicates you're focused and attentive. And marriage experts have found that just making an affirming sound when the other is talking can enhance communication and overall marital satisfaction.

- **Restate your mate's core issue.** Don't assume you always understand the key points your mate is making. He or she may talk for several minutes and you may lose track of their key message. You may want to give a time-out signal to pause the conversation so you can verify your understanding: "Hold on a moment; let me repeat that back to see if I am getting it." Mates can avoid many misunderstandings and also be assured that the other is earnestly listening if each restates what he or she hears the other saying. "Am I hearing this right, you want me to stop trying to fix you when you are upset? You just want me to listen, right? You're not looking for a solution, but you need me to understand your heart?" Your quest is to gain a more intimate understanding of each other. Making sure you understand exactly what your mate is saying gives you important insights into their feelings.

- **Make eye contact, too.** This is often a particularly hard one for men during football season or for some women during bedtime for kids. But it has to be done. Eye-to-eye contact during conversation plays almost as important a role as the words you say. If you "listen" to your mate's eyes, you will understand him or her much better. Are his eyes looking straight at you? Then he's listening. Are her eyes looking away? She may not be engaged in what you're saying. Is he squinting? He hears you but he's skeptical. Are her eyes wide open? She's drinking in every word. If you can learn to read the eyes, you will come to attain a much greater understanding of what your mate is really communicating and how he or she is responding to what you say.

- **Set the scene.** Effective listening requires that you eliminate distractions. Turn off the TV, unplug the phone, and arrange for the kids to be out of your space. Let your mate know that talking, listening, and understanding each other means more to you than anything else at this moment.

What's Next

The last promise might be the promise of greatest importance to God. When you are living it, you are right in the center of his eternal will for you—being a servant to your mate.

SESSION SIX

5th Promise:

I PROMISE TO SERVE YOU ALL THE DAYS OF MY LIFE

Imagine living with a mate who feels called to serve your

deepest needs and dreams—a mate who supports and

cheers for you along your spiritual journey.

CATCHING UP . . . . 10 minutes

- Opening prayer.

- Did you get a chance to read chapter 7 in *I Promise*? Take a few minutes to share your thoughts and insights.

- How did it go this past week when you practiced effective communication? What were some of the results?

- Did you experience conflict or escalation at the levels of opinions, feelings, needs, or beliefs? If so, how did you reach resolution?

Key Verse

For you have been called to live in freedom—not freedom to satisfy your sinful nature, but freedom to serve one another in love.

Galatians 5:13 (NLT)

Watch the video lesson now and take notes in the outline . . . . 20 minutes

5th Promise: I PROMISE TO SERVE YOU ALL THE DAYS OF MY LIFE

SERVING IS THE HIGHEST CALLING IN LIFE

"The greatest among you must be a servant."

(Matthew 23:11 NLT)

[37]Jesus replied, "'You must love the Lord your God with all your heart, all your soul, and all your mind.' [38]This is the first and greatest commandment. [39]A second is equally important: 'Love your neighbor as yourself.' [40]All the other commandments and all the demands of the prophets are based on these two commandments."

(Matthew 22:37–40 NLT)

For you have been called to live in freedom—not freedom to satisfy your sinful nature, but freedom to serve one another in love.

(Galatians 5:13 NLT)

TWO WAYS TO SERVE YOUR MATE

1. Discover your mate's deepest needs.

> *Treat her with understanding as you live together.*
>
> (1 Peter 3:7b NLT)

> [1]*. . . Wives, be submissive to your own husbands so that even if any of them are disobedient to the word, they may be won without a word by the behavior of their wives* [2]*as they observe your chaste and respectful behavior.*
>
> (1 Peter 3:1–2 NASB)

2. Assist your mate on their spiritual journey.

Help him or her discover God's unique calling on their life.

> [3]*Do nothing out of selfish ambition or vain conceit, but in humility consider others better than yourselves.* [4]*Each of you should look not only to your own interests, but also to the interests of others.*
>
> (Philippians 2:3–4 NIV)

God's calling on your life is to serve your mate and to enrich your marriage by serving God together.

> *Greater love has no one than this, that he lay down his life for his friends.*
>
> (John 15:13 NIV)

So here's the ultimate challenge: Try to out-serve your mate! But you won't be able to do it without God's Word and God's Spirit in your heart.

DISCUSSION QUESTIONS . . . . **40 minutes**

1. Take two or three minutes to complete these statements in writing. Then pair up with your spouse and share your responses with him or her.

   I feel loved by you when…

   I feel served by you when…

   Would anyone like to share their responses with the group?

2. To be a servant in marriage you must know your spouse. Genuine serving means learning to identify your husband's or wife's specific needs and looking for creative ways to meet them. How well do you know your mate? Have you made it your goal to study your mate to know and embrace the innermost desires and needs in his or her heart? How can you discover what your mate's needs are?

3. What is one thing you can start doing, or stop doing, from now on that will demonstrate a servant-heart to your spouse?

4. What has this study meant to you? How has it impacted your marriage?

Note from Gary: There are many other resources to help you figure out what your mate's greatest needs may be and how you can meet them, including a couple of my past books, *If Only He Knew* and *For Better or For Best.* Another great resource on this subject is *The Five Love Languages* by Gary Chapman.

LIVING ON PURPOSE . . . . **10 minutes**

MINISTRY

> *And they began to argue among themselves as to who would be the greatest in the coming Kingdom.*
>
> (Luke 22:24 NLT)

Jesus provides the perfect example for developing a life that serves our mate. He was the Lord of the universe, but he showed in his life that the highest calling of a great leader is to be a servant. Luke 22:24 shows his disciples caught up in their own ambition for success and power, arguing over who would be the greatest in the coming kingdom. But Jesus rebuked them saying, *"Those who are the greatest should take the lowest rank, and the leader should be like a servant. Normally the master sits at the table and is served by his servants. But not here! For I am your servant."*

> (Luke 22:26–27 NLT)

Jesus let them in on the secret of true leadership: A true leader looks to the needs of others first and sees that they are met. I, for one, want to be known as a servant.

What would it look like in your life—with your spouse, your family, your coworkers, your friends—to become more like Jesus the servant-leader?

Note from Gary: What comes to mind for me is the picture of Jesus wearing a towel, bent over the dirty feet of those twelve dear friends, washing away the grime of the road. We become most like Christ when we serve.

If you want a happy, fulfilled marriage, you get there not by making a happy marriage your ultimate goal, but by simply becoming more like Christ. Serve your mate selflessly, and you will find lasting joy in marriage. And what's more secure in a marriage than to have a mate whose ultimate goal is to become Christ's servant, which means that your mate will love you unconditionally? That's why my goal in marriage is no longer to be a great husband; it's to be a great servant—because great servants make great marriages. Tuck away in your heart Bible verses like Galatians 5:13 and watch how God will use the power of his Word to begin transforming you into a servant.

PRAYER DIRECTION . . . . 10 minutes

Take a few moments right now to pray and thank Christ for his model of servanthood. Ask him to help you on your journey as you become your mate's biggest champion and ally.

1. During the group prayer time in our first session of this study, you were asked to write a prayer for your spouse and a prayer for yourself (see page 7). Now, as we come to the end of this study, take a few minutes to read silently the prayers you wrote in our first week. Then, in the space below, write a new prayer for your marriage.

2. Take a few minutes in group prayer to thank God for what he is doing in your small group. Thank him for the relationships you have developed and the things you have learned together.

3. Invite couples to share prayer requests as they feel led. Be sure to record these requests in the Small Group Prayer and Praise Report section on pages 77–79 of this study guide. Then pray for each other's requests.

Putting It Into Practice

1. Read the final chapters in *I Promise*.

2. Complete Article V of your *I Promise* Marriage Constitution. (We have included Gary's as an example on the next page.)

I promise . . .

_____

_____

_____

_____

_____

_____

_____

> **GARY'S ARTICLE V**
>
> **I PROMISE to serve you all the days of my life.** I will fight all tendencies toward selfishness in me and focus on keeping you, your needs, and your goals before me at all times. I will continue to hide God's most important words in my heart . . . serving you willingly and wholeheartedly, just as Christ served his disciples not only in small, humble ways but also by giving his life for them and for us as well. (Galatians 5:13)

3. After you have completed Article V, be sure to copy your preamble and all five articles onto a nicely designed, cleanly typed or handwritten paper. Sign your Marriage Constitution and have it framed so you can display it prominently in your home. (You can see Gary's complete *I Promise* Marriage Constitution on page 65 of this study guide.)

What's Next

How can you become a servant of your spouse? Study the following list of needs that Gary has compiled from his years of research and experience. Remember, part of serving is getting inside your mate's heart so you know his or her needs, feelings, beliefs, interests, and tastes intimately.

- *My spouse needs to feel secure, loved, and honored.* My spouse is more valuable to me than my children, my job, my friends, my hobbies, or anything else on this earth.

- *My spouse needs open and unobstructed communication.* I will work hard to develop this in our marriage.

- *My spouse needs my shoulder before my mouth.* Empathy and comfort should precede advice or a solution to the problem.

- *My spouse needs to know I will defend and support her or him.* If what my spouse is doing is indefensible and insupportable, then I will support the potential to change.

- *My spouse needs to be held and touched.* God made us to connect, and meaningful touch is incredibly powerful.

- *My spouse needs to be praised verbally.* Praise shows I notice and appreciate what my mate does. The lack of praise conveys minimal worth.

- *My spouse needs help.* The best help is without commentary on the way the other does things. If I am unsure how to help, I will ask him or her for direction.

- *My spouse needs to share our lives together in every area.* This moves us toward oneness.

- *My spouse needs support when life is falling apart.* Support does not mean lectures and advice. The essence of support is a caring attitude.

- *My spouse needs my prayers, spiritual focus, and transparency about my walk with God.* My relationship with Christ should not be held private from my mate.

I Promise

MARRIAGE CONSTITUTION

PREAMBLE: *When we wed I committed to love and cherish you all the days of my life, and I affirm that commitment today. I love you dearly, more than life itself. I honor you and place you above all other people in my life. My goal is to create in our marriage a place of security in which you and I can share everything in safety and honor without fear, and grow together in deeper love and intimacy. To confirm my commitment to this goal, I willingly make these five solemn promises to you:*

I PROMISE to conform my beliefs to God's truth. I will gain control of my outlook, emotions, and happiness by continually examining my deepest beliefs and striving to make them consistent with what God's Word says. I take sole responsibility for my beliefs, with the understanding that they, not you, determine my emotions, words, thoughts, and actions. Thus, I lift from you the burden of being responsible for any of my ultimate life quality.

I PROMISE to be filled by God. I will keep God in my heart as my source of joy and love. My love for you will be his love flowing through me. And I will receive your love as overflow from him. I will base the security of our marriage on making Christ my boss. I will strive to conform to his image and follow all his commands, especially the one to love you and care for you all the days of my life. (Ephesians 5:25–26, Philippians 4:19)

I PROMISE to find God's best in every trial. I give you the security of knowing that the negative things that happen in our marriage will not destroy my love for you. I will not expect perfection from you, but will use even the irritations between us as opportunities to see my blind spots and foster my personal growth. I will call on the power of Christ to root out my weaknesses. (Romans 8:28, James 1:12, Romans 5:3–5)

I PROMISE to listen and communicate with love. I will value every word you speak as a window to your heart. I will honor your opinions, feelings, needs, and beliefs so that you will feel free to speak honestly and openly with full security in my love for you. I will be open with you in communicating my heart and will consider your feelings and needs in all my words. I will help you solve every disagreement with me until you feel like a winner. (Ephesians 4:29)

I PROMISE to serve you all the days of my life. I will fight all tendencies toward selfishness in me and focus on keeping you, your needs, and your goals before me at all times. I will continue to hide God's most important words in my heart . . . serving you willingly and wholeheartedly, just as Christ served his disciples not only in small, humble ways but also by giving his life for them and for us as well. (Galatians 5:13)

Signed:_____ Date:_____

Signed:_____ Date:_____

Notes

GROUP RESOURCES

I Promise

Helps for Hosts

Top Ten Ideas for New Hosts

Congratulations! As the host of your small group, you have responded to the call to help shepherd Jesus' flock. Few other tasks in the family of God surpass the contribution you will be making. As you prepare to facilitate your group, whether it is one session or the entire series, here are a few thoughts to keep in mind.

Remember you are not alone. God knows everything about you, and he knew you would be asked to facilitate your group. Even though you may not feel ready, this is common for all good hosts. God promises, *"I will never leave you; I will never abandon you"* (Hebrews 13:5 TEV). Whether you are facilitating for one evening, several weeks, or a lifetime, you will be blessed as you serve.

1. **Don't try to do it alone.** Pray right now for God to help you build a healthy team. If you can enlist a co-host to help you shepherd the group, you will find your experience much richer. This is your chance to involve as many people as you can in building a healthy group. All you have to do is ask people to help. You'll be surprised at the response.

2. **Be friendly and be yourself.** God wants to use your unique gifts and temperament. Be sure to greet people at the door with a big smile . . . this can set the mood for the whole gathering. Remember, they are taking as big a step as you are to show up at your house! Don't try to do things exactly like another host; do them in a way that fits you. Admit when you don't have an answer and apologize when you make a mistake. Your group will love you for it and you'll sleep better at night.

3. **Prepare for your meeting ahead of time.** Review the session and write down your responses to each question. Pay special attention to exercises that ask group members to do something other than engage in discussion. These exercises will help your group live what the Bible teaches, not just talk about it. Be sure you understand how an exercise works. If the exercise employs one of the items in the Group Resources section (such as the Purpose Driven Group Guidelines), be sure to look over that item so you'll know how it works.

4. **Pray for your group members by name.** Before you begin your session, take a few moments and pray for each member by name. You may want to review the prayer list at least once a week. Ask God to use your time together to touch the heart of every person in your group. Expect God to lead you to whomever he wants you to encourage or challenge in a special way. If you listen, God will surely lead.

5. **When you ask a question, be patient.** Someone will eventually respond. Sometimes people need a moment or two of silence to think about the question. If silence doesn't bother you, it won't bother anyone else. After someone responds, affirm the response with a simple "thanks" or "great answer." Then ask, "How about somebody else?" or "Would someone who hasn't shared like to add anything?" Be sensitive to new people or reluctant members who aren't ready to say, pray, or do anything. If you give them a safe setting, they will blossom over time. If someone in your group is a "wall flower" who sits silently through every session, consider talking to them privately and encouraging them to participate. Let them know how important they are to you—that they are loved and appreciated, and that the group would value their input. Remember, still water often runs deep.

6. **Provide transitions between questions.** Ask if anyone would like to read the paragraph or Bible passage. Don't call on anyone, but ask for a volunteer, and then be patient until someone begins. Be sure to thank the person who reads aloud.

7. **Break into smaller groups occasionally.** With a greater opportunity to talk in a small circle, people will connect more with the study, apply more quickly what they're learning, and ultimately get more out of their small group experience. A small circle also encourages a quiet person to participate and tends to minimize the effects of a more vocal or dominant member.

8. **Small circles are also helpful during prayer time.** People who are unaccustomed to praying aloud will feel more comfortable trying it with just two or three others. Also, prayer requests won't take as much time, so circles will have more time to actually pray. When you gather back with the whole group, you can have one person from each circle briefly update everyone on the prayer requests from their subgroups. The other great aspect of subgrouping is that it fosters leadership development. As you ask people in the group to facilitate discussion or to lead a prayer circle, it gives them a small leadership step that can build their confidence.

9. **Rotate facilitators occasionally.** You may be perfectly capable of hosting each time, but you will help others grow in their faith and gifts if you give them opportunities to host the group.

10. **One final challenge (for new or first-time hosts).** Before your first opportunity to lead, look up each of the five passages listed below. Read each one as a devotional exercise to help prepare you with a shepherd's heart. Trust us on this one. If you do this, you will be more than ready for your first meeting.

Matthew 9:36–38 (NIV)

[36]When Jesus saw the crowds, he had compassion on them, because they were harassed and helpless, like sheep without a shepherd. [37]Then he said to his disciples, "The harvest is plentiful but the workers are few. [38]Ask the Lord of the harvest, therefore, to send out workers into his harvest field."

John 10:14–15 (NIV)

[14]I am the good shepherd; I know my sheep and my sheep know me—[15]just as the Father knows me and I know the Father—and I lay down my life for the sheep.

1 Peter 5:2–4 (NIV)

[2]Be shepherds of God's flock that is under your care, serving as overseers—not because you must, but because you are willing, as God wants you to be; [3]not greedy for money, but eager to serve; not lording it over those entrusted to you, but being examples to the flock. [4]And when the Chief Shepherd appears, you will receive the crown of glory that will never fade away.

Philippians 2:1–5 (NIV)

[1]If you have any encouragement from being united with Christ, if any comfort from his love, if any fellowship with the Spirit, if any tenderness and compassion, [2]then make my joy complete by being like-minded, having the same love, being one in spirit and purpose. [3]Do nothing out of selfish ambition or vain conceit, but in humility consider others better than yourselves. [4]Each of you should look not only to your own interests, but also to the interests of others. [5]Your attitude should be the same as that of Jesus Christ.

Hebrews 10:23–25 (NIV)

[23]Let us hold unswervingly to the hope we profess, for he who promised is faithful. [24]And let us consider how we may spur one another on toward love and good deeds. [25]Let us not give up meeting together, as some are in the habit of doing, but let us encourage one another—and all the more as you see the Day approaching.

1 Thessalonians 2:7–8, 11–12 (NIV)

[7]. . . but we were gentle among you, like a mother caring for her little children. [8]We loved you so much that we were delighted to share with you not only the Gospel of God but our lives as well, because you had become so dear to us. . . . [11]For you know that we dealt with each of you as a father deals with his own children, [12]encouraging, comforting and urging you to live lives worthy of God, who calls you into his kingdom and glory.

Frequently Asked Questions

How long will this group meet?

I Promise is six sessions long. We encourage your group to add a seventh session for a celebration. In your final session, each group member may decide if he or she desires to continue on for another study. At that time you may also want to do some informal evaluation, discuss your group guidelines, and decide which study you want to do next. We recommend you visit our website at **www.purposedriven.com** for more video-based small group studies.

Who is the host?

The host is the person who coordinates and facilitates your group meetings. In addition to a host, we encourage you to select one or more group members to lead your group discussions. Several other responsibilities can be rotated, including refreshments, prayer requests, worship, or keeping up with those who miss a meeting. Shared ownership in the group helps everybody grow.

Where do we find new group members?

Recruiting new members can be a challenge for groups, especially new groups with just a few people, or existing groups that lose a few people along the way. We encourage you to use the Circles of Life diagram on page 76 of this workbook to brainstorm a list of people from your workplace, church, school, neighborhood, family, and so on. Then pray for the people on each member's list. Allow each member to invite several people from their list. Some groups fear that newcomers will interrupt the intimacy that members have built over time. However, groups that welcome newcomers generally gain strength with the infusion of new blood. Remember, the next person you add just might become a friend for eternity. Logistically, groups find different ways to add members. Some groups remain permanently open, while others choose to open periodically, such as at the beginning or end of a study. If your group becomes too large for easy, face-to-face conversations, you can subgroup, forming a second discussion group in another room.

How do we handle the childcare needs in our group?

Childcare needs must be handled very carefully. This is a sensitive issue. We suggest you seek creative solutions as a group. One common solution is to have the adults meet in the living room and share the cost of a baby sitter (or two) who can be with the kids in another part of the house. Another popular option is to have one home for the kids and a second home (close by) for the adults. If desired, the adults could rotate the responsibility of providing a lesson for the kids. This last option is great with school age kids and can be a huge blessing to families.

Purpose Driven Group Guidelines

It's a good idea for every group to put words to their shared values, expectations, and commitments. Such guidelines will help you avoid unspoken agendas and unmet expectations. We recommend you discuss your guidelines during Session One in order to lay the foundation for a healthy group experience. Feel free to modify anything that does not work for your group.

We agree to the following values:

Clear Purpose	To grow healthy spiritual lives by building a healthy small group community
Group Attendance	To give priority to the group meeting (call if I am absent or late)
Safe Environment	To create a safe place where people can be heard and feel loved (no quick answers, snap judgments, or simple fixes)
Be Confidential	To keep anything that is shared strictly confidential and within the group
Conflict Resolution	To avoid gossip and to immediately resolve any concerns by following the principles of Matthew 18:15–17
Spiritual Health	To give group members permission to speak into my life and help me live a healthy, balanced spiritual life that is pleasing to God
Limit Our Freedom	To limit our freedom by not serving or consuming alcohol during small group meetings or events so as to avoid causing a weaker brother or sister to stumble (1 Corinthians 8:1–13; Romans 14:19–21)
Welcome Newcomers	To invite friends who might benefit from this study and warmly welcome newcomers
Building Relationships	To get to know the other members of the group and pray for them regularly
Other	_____

We have also discussed and agree on the following items:

Child Care

_____

_____

Starting Time

_____

Ending Time

_____

If you haven't already done so, take a few minutes to fill out the Small Group Calendar on page 80.

Circles of Life: SMALL GROUP CONNECTIONS

Discover who you can connect in community

Use this chart to help carry out one of the values in the Purpose Driven Group Guidelines, to "Welcome Newcomers."

"Follow me, and I will make you fishers of men."

(Matthew 4:19 KJV)

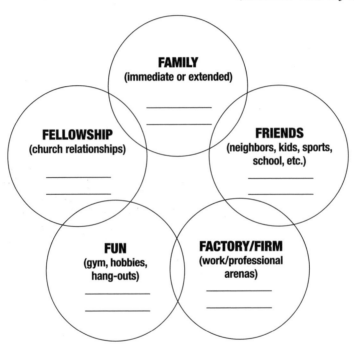

FAMILY
(immediate or extended)

FELLOWSHIP
(church relationships)

FRIENDS
(neighbors, kids, sports, school, etc.)

FUN
(gym, hobbies, hang-outs)

FACTORY/FIRM
(work/professional arenas)

Follow this simple three-step process:

1. List one to two people in each circle.

2. Prayerfully select one person or couple from your list and tell your group about them.

3. Give them a call and invite them to your next meeting. Over fifty percent of those invited to a small group say, "Yes!"

Small Group Prayer and Praise Report

This is a place where you can write each other's requests for prayer. You can also make a note when God answers a prayer. Pray for each other's requests. If you're new to group prayer, it's okay to pray silently or to pray by using just one sentence:

"God, please help _____ to _____ ."

DATE	PERSON	PRAYER REQUEST	PRAISE REPORT

Small Group Prayer and Praise Report

DATE	PERSON	PRAYER REQUEST	PRAISE REPORT

Small Group Prayer and Praise Report

DATE	PERSON	PRAYER REQUEST	PRAISE REPORT

Small Group Calendar

Healthy groups share responsibilities and group ownership. It might take some time for this to develop. Shared ownership ensures that responsibility for the group doesn't fall to one person. Use the calendar to keep track of social events, mission projects, birthdays, or days off. Complete this calendar at your first or second meeting. Planning ahead will increase attendance and shared ownership.

DATE	LESSON	LOCATION	FACILITATOR	SNACK OR MEAL
10/22	Session 2	Steve and Laura	Bill Jones	John and Alice

Key Verses

One of the most effective ways to drive deeply into our lives the principles we are learning in this series is to memorize key scriptures. For many, memorization is a new concept or one that has been difficult in the past. We encourage you to stretch yourself and try to memorize five key verses. If possible, memorize these as a group and make them part of your group time. You may cut these apart and carry them in your wallet.

I have hidden your word in my heart that I might not sin against you.

Psalm 119:11 (NIV)

Session One *How precious are your thoughts about me, O God! They are innumerable! I can't even count them; they outnumber the grains of sand!* Psalm 139:17–18a (NLT)	**Session Two** *Above all else, guard your heart, for it is the wellspring of life.* Proverbs 4:23 (NIV)
Session Three *Without faith it is impossible to please God, because anyone who comes to him must believe that he exists and he rewards those who earnestly seek him.* Hebrews 11:6 (NIV)	**Session Four** *We can rejoice, too, when we run into problems and trials, for we know that they are good for us—they help us learn to endure.* Romans 5:3 (NLT)
Session Five *Do not let any unwholesome talk come out of your mouths, but only what is helpful in building others up according to their needs, that it may benefit those who listen.* Ephesians 4:29 (NIV)	**Session Six** *For you have been called to live in freedom—not freedom to satisfy your sinful nature, but freedom to serve one another in love.* Galatians 5:13 (NLT)

Dr. Gary Smalley is the founder and chairman of the Smalley Relationship Center and the author and co-author of more than forty marriage & parenting books, including the best-selling *Making Love Last Forever, The Blessing, The DNA of Relationships,* and the award-winning *Redemption* fiction series (with Karen Kingsbury). Gary has appeared on national television programs such as *The Oprah Winfrey Show, Larry King Live,* and the *Today Show* as well as numerous national radio programs. As a speaker, he has spoken to millions of people in over 100 major cities in the US as well as countries all over the world. Gary and his wife, Norma, have been married for forty-one years and live in Branson, Missouri. They have three children and eight grandchildren.

The Smalley Relationship Center provides conferences and resources for couples, singles, parents, and churches. The Center captures research, connects people to counseling options, and develops new tools for those building relationships. To find out more about Gary Smalley's speaking schedule, conferences, and to receive a weekly e-letter with articles and coaching ideas on your relationships, go to www.garysmalley.com.

I Promise

A Life-Changing Marriage Book, designed to be read with the I Promise *Study!*

In the book *I Promise,* Dr. Gary Smalley uses humor, practical insights, years of research, and biblical principles to communicate 5 key commitments that determine the destiny of your marriage.

Dr. Smalley has narrowed the core biblical principles into 5 Promises. Each promise is designed to make spouses feel safe, highly valued, and committed for life!

Dr. Smalley has over 11 million resources in print and has been on national media for years. Founder of the Smalley Relationship Center, Dr. Smalley has spent years discovering biblical breakthroughs that are extremely effective for most couples!

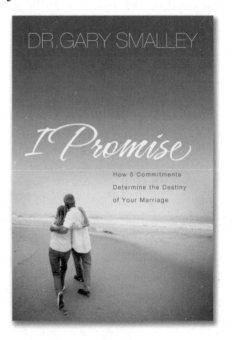

Included are:

- 5 core promises that build a relationship where you are secure and unconditionally loved.

- 3 powerful ways to improve your relationship with God.

- Learn the biggest marriage mistake that most couples make.

- Discover why marital trials and irritations are the secret to intimacy needs.

40 Days of Purpose
Small Group Edition

Based on the best-selling book, *The Purpose Driven®
Life* by Rick Warren, this curriculum is uniquely
designed for church members and new believers who
desire to fulfill God's purpose for their lives.

40 Days of Purpose Small Group Edition is also
great for those who want to review the material
in their new or existing small group/class, share it
with a friend, or even for pastors who want to
review the five purposes with their church family.

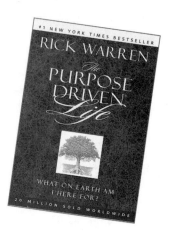

To order product or for more information please visit:
www.purposedriven.com or call 1.800.723.3532

S.H.A.P.E.

Find & Fulfill Your Unique Purpose for Life

In his book, *The Purpose Driven® Life*, Rick Warren introduced the concept of S.H.A.P.E.—Spiritual gifts, Heart, Abilities, Personality, Experiences— and showed us how God uses our unique S.H.A.P.E. to release us into ministry.

In this video-based small group study, Erik Rees builds on Rick Warren's foundational teaching by taking you through the process of discovering your own personal S.H.A.P.E.—the remarkable elements that work together to make you who you are, and that point you to the life-purpose God has planned just for you.

Discover God's most powerful and effective means of advancing his kingdom: You! Learn how God can use your own irreplaceable, richly detailed, personal S.H.A.P.E., empowered by the Holy Spirit, to accomplish his purposes on the earth!

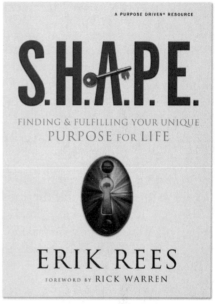

- Unlock your God-given potential!

- Uncover your specific kingdom purpose!

- Unfold a kingdom plan for your life!

You are uniquely S.H.A.P.E.d to bring glory to God. Find out how, through this life-changing small group study.

Available now at *www.purposedriven.com.*

The Way of a Worshiper

The pursuit of God is the chase of a lifetime—in fact, it's been going on since the day you were born. The question is: Have you been the hunter or the prey?

This small group study is not about music. It's not even about going to church. It's about living your life as an offering of worship to God. It's about tapping into the source of power to live the Christian life. And it's about discovering the secret to friendship with God.

In these four video sessions, Buddy Owens helps you unpack the meaning of worship. Through his very practical, engaging, and at times surprising insights, Buddy shares truths from Scripture and from life that will help you understand in a new and deeper way just what it means to be a worshiper.

God is looking for worshipers. His invitation to friendship is open and genuine. Will you take him up on his offer? Will you give yourself to him in worship? Then come walk the Way of a Worshiper and discover the secret to friendship with God.

THE WAY of a WORSHIPER

Your study of this material will be greatly enhanced by reading the book, *The Way of a Worshiper: Discover the Secret to Friendship with God.*

To order product or for more information please visit:
www.purposedriven.com or call 1.800.723.3532

Inside Out Living

In the Sermon on the Mount, Jesus reaches beneath our actions to the attitudes that motivate us. He teaches us how to stop living for ourselves, and how to start living beyond ourselves. And that kind of living is Inside Out Living. Small groups will find this three-volume study to be challenging, practical, at times controversial, and always quite surprising.

What Jesus Has to Say About Living a Blessed Life

Pastor Lance Witt of Saddleback Church will engage groups in an enriching, verse-by-verse discussion of the Beatitudes, and living as salt and light as found in Matthew 5:1–16.

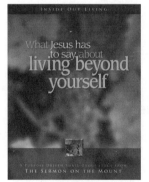

What Jesus Has to Say About Living Beyond Yourself

The primary focus of this volume is relationships, and it includes Jesus' teaching on anger management, faithfulness in marriage, being both truthful and trustworthy, and loving our enemies.

What Jesus Has to Say About Living in Pursuit of God

Six, in-depth, verse-by-verse studies of Jesus' teaching on the Lord's Prayer, fasting, materialism, and storing up treasures in Heaven.

Managing Our Finances God's Way

A dynamic new small group study featuring five renowned experts!

Introducing a new video-based small group study that will inspire you to live debt free! This seven-week study created by Purpose Driven and Crown Financial Ministries features five renowned experts on the subject of biblical financial management.

Learn what the Bible has to say about our finances from Rick Warren, Chip Ingram, Ron Blue, Howard Dayton, and Chuck Bentley in this new video-based small group study. Plus, get practical tools to help you manage your finances and live debt free.

Study includes:

- DVD with seven 20-minute lessons
- Workbook with seven lessons
- Resource CD with digital version of all worksheets that perform calculations automatically
- Contact information for help with answering questions
- Resources for keeping financial plans on track and making them lifelong habits

> NOTE: PARTICIPANTS DO NOT SHARE PERSONAL FINANCIAL INFORMATION WITH EACH OTHER.

To order product or for more information please visit:
www.purposedriven.com or call 1.800.723.3532